Library of Congress Catalog Card Number: 62-8585
Printed in the United States of America

E

LET'S FIND OUT ABOUT

WHEELS

by

MARTHA and CHARLES SHAPP

Pictures by Peter Costanza

FRANKLIN WATTS, INC.
575 Lexington Avenue, New York 22

Wheels, wheels, wheels!
Big wheels, small wheels, middle-sized wheels!

Wheels help us in many ways.

Wheels help us go places.
There are wheels on cars.

There are wheels on planes.

Wheels help carry things from place to place.
There are wheels on trucks.

There are wheels on trains.

Wheels make work easier.
It's not easy to carry a heavy load.

Wheels make carrying easier.

It's not easy to lift a heavy load.

Wheels make lifting easier.

Digging is hard work.

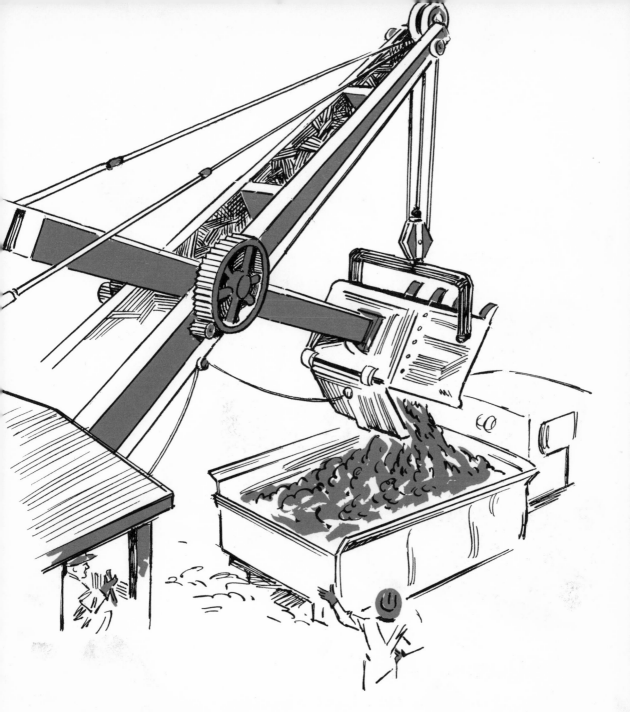

Wheels make digging easier.

Wheels help us have fun.
Toy trains and cars have wheels.

Doll carriages have wheels.

Skates have wheels.

Bikes have wheels.

Have you ever had a ride on this wheel?

Have you ever had a ride on this wheel?

Wheels help at home.
Wheels help mother sew.

Wheels help mother keep the house clean.

Wheels help father mow the lawn.

Wheels help father keep the yard clean.

Wheels help in the city . . .

. . . and in the country.

Long, long ago there were no wheels.

Pulling a heavy load was hard work.

One day somebody happened to pull a heavy load over a log.
The log rolled.

The rolling log made it easier to pull the load.

Soon many people used logs to help move heavy loads.

Soon somebody thought of an easier way.
He used part of the log instead of the whole log.

He had made the first wheel!

Now there are many, many wheels of all kinds.

Some wheels are tiny.

Some wheels are big.
But all wheels are round.

Round and round go the wheels.

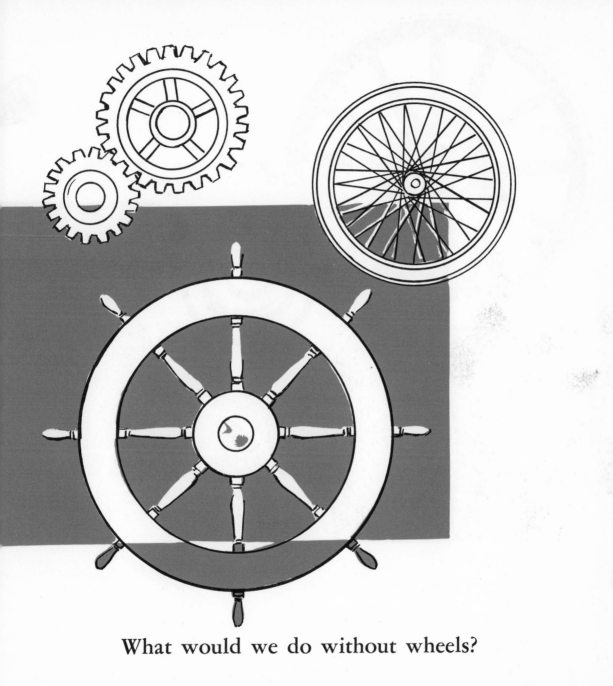

What would we do without wheels?

VOCABULARY LIST (100 words)

a
ago
all
an
and
are
at

bikes
big
but

carriages
carry (ing)
cars
city
clean
country

day
digging
do
doll

easier
easy
ever

father
first
from
fun

go

had
happened
hard
have
he

heavy
help
home
house

in
instead
is
it ('s)

keep
kinds

lawn
lift (ing)
log
long
look

made
make
many
middle-sized
mother
move
mow

no
not
now

of
on
one
over

part
people
place (s)
planes

pull (ing)

ride
roll (ed) (ing)
round

sew
skates
small
some
somebody
soon

the
there
things
this
thought
tiny
to
toy
trains
trucks

us
used

was
way (s)
we
were
what
wheels
whole
without
work
would

yard
you